Royal Families Worldwide
A Gazetteer

Royal Families Worldwide

A Gazetteer

MARK WATSON

SHEPHEARD-WALWYN

First published 1999 by
Shepheard-Walwyn (Publishers) Ltd
26 Charing Cross Road (Suite 34)
London WC2H 0DH

British Library Cataloguing in Publication Data

A catalogue record of this book
is available from the British Library

ISBN 085683 170 0

Typeset by R E Clayton
Printed in Malta by Interprint Ltd

Contents

Acknowledgements

The author and publisher wish to express their gratitude to the copyright owners listed below for permission to reproduce the following photographs:

Royal households: Albania, King Leka; Belgium, King Albert & Queen Paola; Brazil, Dom Luiz; Bulgaria, King Simeon; Burma, Prince Shewbomin; Ethiopia, Princes Ermias and Bekere; Germany (Bavaria), Duke Franz; Greece, King Constantine; Libya, Prince Idris; Liechtenstein, Prince Hans-Adam; Luxembourg, Grand Duke Jean; Monaco, Prince Rainier; Nepal, King Birendra; Rwanda, King Kigeli; Uganda (Buganda), Kabaka Mutebi; Uganda (Bunyoro-Kitara), King Solomon; Uganda (Toro), King Rukidi; Yugoslavia, Prince Alexander;

Embassies or High Commissions: Bahrain, Shaikh Hamad; Cambodia, King Sihanouk; Denmark, Queen Margarethe; Japan, Emperor Akihito; Jordan, King Abdullah; Kuwait, Amir Jabir; Lesotho, King Letsie; Malaysia, The Yang di-Pertuan Agong; Morocco, King Hassan; Netherlands, Queen Beatrix; Norway, King Harald; Oman, Sultan Qaboos; Qatar, Sheikh Hamad; Spain, King Juan Carlos; Swaziland, King Mswati; Sweden, King Carl; Thailand, King Bhumibol; Tonga, King Tupou; United Arab Emirates, Sheikh Zayed;

Associated Press: Bhutan, King Jigme; Brunei, Sultan Haji; Romania, King Michael; Saudi Arabia, King Fahd;

Camera Press; United Kingdom, Queen Elizabeth;

Frank Spooner Pictures: Austria-Hungary, Archduke Otto; France (Royal), Prince Henri; Italy, Prince Vittorio Emanuele; Russia, Grand Duke George;

Media Sud News: France (Imperial), Prince Charles.

Finally the author and publisher wish to acknowledge the helpful assistance they have received from private secretaries and embassies in the research for this book and express the hope that cooperation may continue into future editions.

Publisher's Note

We are aware that not all royal families in the world have been included in this the first edition of *Royal Families Worldwide*. Some families have chosen not to be included and we have respected their wishes, but it is our hope that, once they have seen this first edition, they will recognise that there is no intention of intruding into their privacy. The purpose is essentially to provide accurate information and to educate.

The arrangement is alphabetical by country, but some countries have been allocated more than two pages, either because there are rival claimants to the throne, as in France, or because within an existing modern state there is more than one ancient royal family, such as Germany or Uganda.

For ease of reference and comparison with other countries, we have set out the material under standard headings. This has revealed different cultural attitudes to the disclosure of information about family members and birth dates. We have sought to respect that by stating that the information is not publicly available.

Modern Monarchy

This book is about monarchy, in some cases thriving, in others waiting in the wings: but there is general consensus that where it does thrive in a particular state, it stands for a settled, orderly method of government. Increasingly, in this modern age, constitutional monarchy exists in contrast with strong, autocratic presidential systems, as republics and monarchies rub along together. Presidential systems may be orderly enough; but they are prone to excessive ambition, greed and outright corruption.

Plato, who of all ancient philosophers seems to speak to us today in a way we all understand, argued that moderation was the key to monarchical success: a light hand on the tiller of the state. Elected presidents tend to be heavy-handed, wanting to achieve historical significance for their acts, and knowing they have a limited time in which to prove themselves. An American president, for example, has about a hundred days from initial election to realise his personal goals: after that honeymoon period he is working for re-election, and in the second term of office he is - to mix the metaphors - a lame duck.

Monarchs, on the other hand, have time on their side, and a family to carry forward their good works. They have freedom to look forward and to look back, connecting history, traditions and customs with a sound future for their peoples. They are not necessarily burdened with the political events of the day, leaving those to the politicians. They must be watchful, of course; they must guard the constitution; but their true merit lies in conducting their peoples into safe paths. King Juan Carlos of Spain is a good example of a monarch who, arriving at a period of great tension in the affairs of his country, has with a light touch on the reins given purpose and direction to his kingdom. When, on a weekend in August 1993, King Baudouin of Belgium died, it was not a meeting of European Finance Ministers which caught the headlines, but the crowds of Belgians swarming to the palace to acknowledge their loss of a king, *le roi triste*, who by dint of personal effort had maintained their fragile unity as a state.

Unity, of course, is most precious. We can be united in a King or Queen. He or she embodies the nation, symbolises it, supplies an emotional want which is as old as mankind. Frequently monarchs are consecrated to their task, by religious ceremonies, which remind them of their great responsibilities, 'under God and the law', and give them the inner, spiritual strength to devote their lives to their people. Education within a continuous family is important here: monarchs are trained and dedicated, unlike political presidents who arrive at the seat of power with nothing to commend them but their own driving ambition for personal success. In many of the increasingly autocratic and lengthy presidencies we see around us today, there is no sense of continuity with the past, and no real hope for the future when, at last, the worn-out occupant departs.

Walter Bagehot, the great 19th century constitutionalist, wrote; 'A *family* on the throne is an interesting idea. It brings down the pride of sovereignty to the level of petty life... A princely marriage is the brilliant edition of a universal fact, and, as such, it rivets mankind'. We smile affectionately when we read, herein, that the present monarch of Thailand is known to his people as the 'Farmer King' because of his interests in agriculture and water supply. They supply a common touch to elegance; but, as well, these studies are concerned with the fundamental needs of a nation. According to the Constitution of the Netherlands, promulgated in 1814, the King was the 'high authority' in all matters connected with water! People put their trust in a monarch; but when they put their trust in a president they can be sadly disillusioned, as happens all too frequently.

Modern monarchy, at its best, is creative, forward-looking and stimulating. Take the present Prince of Wales, for example. Through various trusts and business initiatives, he has actually helped to create work and employment for over 100,000 young people. The Prince has supported a return to basic educational principles, including a love for the language and its greatest exponent, Shakespeare. Whatever one thinks of his views on architecture, he has at least won recognition of the need to consult ordinary people when there are plans afoot to change the skyline. And he has reminded architects that a major part of their function is to create a sense of space and stillness, not to indulge in torments of mind and perspective. In agriculture, he works unceasingly to promote methods which do not result in poisoning ourselves.

For most of this century democracy has been extolled as the best form of government and monarchy has been regarded as undemocratic and old fashioned - at least in intellectual circles. However, the history of the century has shown that democracy in itself is no guarantee of greater justice and social harmony. On the contrary, in those countries where the monarchy has been retained as a part of the constitution, greater political stability has been enjoyed, and in Spain, the reinstatement of monarchy played an important part in the successful restoration of democracy following years of totalitarian rule.

Many of the royal families described in this book are families-in-waiting. Their thrones are vacant. This vacuum at the heart of a state is demonstrated by Paris, where the imperial dimensions of buildings and squares look lost without a prince to complete them. But the fact is, royal families do exist and they can step in when people are mature enough, or have suffered enough, to desire the return of monarchy. Self-respect applies to states as well as individuals - when we respect ourselves sufficiently we call to mind all those qualities symbolised by monarchy: consciousness, brilliance, tradition, intelligence, reason, lawfulness and compassion. This book serves a most important purpose in identifying royal families which remain ready to serve their peoples; and whose restoration would result, in most cases, in the shining forth of these qualities.

By L L Blake

L L Blake is a barrister, author and lecturer, His most recent book is *The Prince and the Professor.*

Albania

Short Title	HM King Leka I
Born	5 April 1939, Tirana
Parents	HM King Zog I of the Albanians
	HM Queen Geraldine of the Albanians
	(née Countess Geraldine Apponyi de Nagy-Appony)
Siblings	None
Religion	Muslim
Married	7 October 1975
Consort	HM Queen Susan of the Albanians
	(née Susan Cullen-Ward)
Children	HRH Crown Prince Leka, 26 March 1982
Residence	Johannesburg, South Africa
Succeeded	11 April 1961 (sworn in)
Status	King of the Albanians (in exile)
Income	Private

The Dynasty

The present claimant King Leka is a direct descendant of Zogu the Great (late 15th century). Zogu the Great emigrated from northern Albania to Mati in the central region of the country, where he led a successful uprising against Turkish rule. Although a Christian at birth, Zogu the Great embraced Islam and his descendants were recognised as Hereditary Governors of Mati. Until 1913 Albania remained under Turkish rule but with varying degrees of independence. During and immediately after the First World War Albania was controlled by different foreign forces. In 1925 Ahmed Bey Zogu emerged as the country's ruler when he was elected President. On 1 December 1928 he assumed the title King Zog. When Italy invaded Albania in April 1939, King Zog fled to Greece and the family went into exile. King Leka is now resident in South Africa and is a successful independent businessman.

HM King Leka I

Austria-Hungary

Short Title	HIRH Archduke Otto, Crown Prince of Austria and Hungary (uncrowned King until 1945), Royal Prince of Bohemia
Born	20 November 1912, Villa Wartholz, Reichenau an der Rax, Austria
Parents	HIRM Emperor and King Karl I HIRM Empress and Queen Zita (née HRH Princess Zita of Bourbon-Parma)
Siblings	None
Religion	Roman Catholic
Married	10 May 1951
Consort	HIRH Archduchess Regina, Crown Princess of Austria and Hungary, Royal Princess of Bohemia (née HRH Princess Regina of Saxe-Meiningen)
Children	HIRH Archduchess Andrea, 30 March 1953 (married Count Eugen of Neipperg) HIRH Archduchess Monika, 13 September 1954 (married HSH Duke of San Angelo) HIRH Archduchess Michaela, 13 September 1954 (married Eric Alba Teran d'Antin) HIRH Archduchess Gabriela, 14 October 1956 (married Christian Meister) HIRH Archduchess Walburga, 6 October 1958 (married Archibald, Count Douglas) HIRH Archduke Karl, (Heir) 1961 (married Baroness Francesca Thyssen-Bornemisza) HIRH Archduke Paul Georg, 16 December 1964 (married HRH Eilika Duchess of Oldenburg)
Residence	Pöcking, Bavaria
Succeeded	1 April 1922
Status	Head of the imperial and royal family
Income	Private

The Dynasty

The family derives its name from the Castle of Habsburg and the line of descent can be traced back to Albert, Count of Habsburg in 1153.

HIRH Archduke Otto

Archduke Otto of Austria, the present head of the Imperial and Royal House of Austria-Hungary is a descendant of the Habsburg Holy Roman Emperor, Rudolf I (1278-91). The family held the title of Holy Roman Emperor until 1806, when Franz II, anticipating the break-up of the Empire, took the title Franz I of Austria. The Ausgleich of 1867 created the Dual Monarchy of Austria - Hungary; the union was dissolved in 1918. The defeat of the Austro-Hungarian Empire in the First World War led to the voluntary exile of Emperor Karl I. At his death in 1922, Archduke Otto succeeded to the imperial and royal titles of Austria, Hungary (uncrowned King till 1945) and Bohemia. Today as a Member of the European Parliament Dr. Otto von Habsburg discourages the use of his family's titles.

Bahrain

Short Title	HH Shaikh Hamad bin Isa Al-Khalifa
Born	28 January 1950, Bahrain
Parents	HH Shaikh Isa bin Sulman Al-Khalifa
Siblings	HH Shaikh Rashid bin Isa
	HH Shaikh Mohammed bin Isa
	HH Shaikh Ali bin Isa
Religion	Muslim
Married	1969
Consort	HH Shaikh Sabeka Al-Khalifa
Children	3 sons, 1 daughter
Residence	Bahrain
Succeeded	6 March 1999
Status	Amir of the State of Bahrain
Income	Private

The Dynasty

The Al-Khalifa family can be traced back to Shaikh Ahmed Al-Fateh (the Conqueror) who took control of Bahrain from the Persians at the end of the 18th century. The seventh Al-Khalifa ruler, Shaikh Isa, succeeded in 1869 at the age of 21. During his long reign, which lasted until his death in 1932, he introduced new and improved administrative and legal institutions and oversaw the foundation of a modern education system. After almost a century as a British Protectorate, the country became an independent state in 1971. The present Shaikh succeeded on the death of his father in 1999.

HH Shaikh Hamad bin Isa Al-Khalifa

Belgium

Short Title	HM King Albert II
Born	6 June 1934, Brussels
Parents	HM King Léopold III
	HM Queen Astrid (née HRH Princess Astrid of Sweden)
Siblings	HRH Princess Josephine-Charlotte, 11 October 1927
	King Baudouin, 7 September 1930 (deceased)
Religion	Roman Catholic
Married	2 July 1959
Consort	HM Queen Paola (née Donna Paola Ruffo di Calabria)
Children	HRH Prince Philippe, 15 April 1960
	HRH Princess Astrid, 5 June 1962
	HRH Prince Laurent, 19 October 1963
Residence	Palace Royale, Brussels
Succeeded	9 August 1993 (on the death of his brother)
Status	Head of state
Income	State

The Dynasty

The Saxe-Coburg-Gotha family have been the royal family of Belgium since 1831 when Leopold I (1790-1865) accepted the crown of this newly independent country, which had broken away from the Kingdom of the Netherlands following a revolution in 1830. His son, King Leopold II (1835-1909), was also King of Congo, during the years that it was a separate independent state. King Albert I (1875-1934) was thought to have led his country through the difficult years of the First World War with success. However, his son King Léopold III (1901-83), who ordered the capitulation of the Belgian Army to the Nazis on 28 May 1940, was blamed for his action. He abdicated in 1951 in favour of his son Baudouin. The current monarch, King Albert II, succeeded on the death of his brother in August 1993.

HM King Albert II and HM Queen Paola

Bhutan

Short Title	HM King Jigme Singye Wangchuck
Born	11 November 1955, Dechencholing Palace, Thimphu
Parents	HM King Jigme Dorji Wangchuck
	HM Ashi Kesang Choeden Wangchuck
Siblings	HRH Ashi Sonam Chodron Wangchuck
	HRH Ashi Dechan Wangmo Wangchuck
	HRH Ashi Pema Lhaden Wangchuck
	HRH Ashi Kesang Wangmo Wangchuck
Religion	Mahayana Buddhism
Married	April 1979
Consort	HM Ashi Dorji Wangmo Wangchuck
	HM Ashi Tshering Pem Wangchuck
	HM Ashi Tshering Yangdon Wangchuck
	HM Ashi Sangay Choden Wangchuck
Children	HRH Dasho Jigmie Khesar Namgyel Wangchuck, 1980
	HRH Ashi Chimi Yangzom Wangchuck, 1980
	HRH Ashi Sonam Dechen Wangchuck, 1981
	HRH Ashi Kesang Choden Wangchuck 1982
	HRH Dasho Jigyel Ugyen Wangchuck, 1984
	HRH Dasho Khamsum Singye Wangchuck, 1985
	HRH Dasho Jigmi Dorji Wangchuck, 1986
	HRH Ashi Eeuphelma Choden Wangchuck, 1993
	HRH Dasho Ugyen Jigme Wangchuck, 1994
Residence	Samtenling, Thimphu
Succeeded	21 June 1972
Status	Head of state and government
Income	State

The Dynasty

The monarchy was established on 17th December 1907 when the clergy, state councillors and governors elected Tongsa Penlop Ugyen

HM King Jigme Singye Wangchuck

Wangchuck as the first King of Bhutan. The present monarch King Jigme Singye Wangchuck is the fourth ruler. He succeeded his father in 1972.

Brazil

Short Title	HIRH Dom Luiz Orléans e Bragança
Born	6 June 1938, São Paulo
Parents	Dom Pedro Henrique Orléans e Bragança
	Dona Maria Elisabeth of Bavaria
Siblings	Eudes, 1939
	Isabelle, 1944
	Pierre, 1945
	Ferdinand, 1948
	Antonine, 1950
	Elenore, 1953
	François, 1955
	Albert, 1957
	Marie-Thérèse, 1959
	Marie Gabrielle 1959
Religion	Roman Catholic
Married	Single
Consort	
Children	
Residence	São Paulo
Succeeded	5 July 1981
Status	Head of the imperial family
Income	Private

The Dynasty

The present head of the imperial family is a descendant of João IV who reigned from 1640 (he was also King of Portugal). Pedro II was deposed in 1889 by a military revolt, the Imperial Family were exiled and monarchists were outlawed. In 1908 the bachelor Head of the Imperial House, Pedro di Alcantara renounced his claim to the throne (and that of any future children). He returned to Brazil in 1931, 10 years after Congress had revoked the banishment of the imperial family. The role

HIRH Dom Luiz Orléans e Bragança

of head of the imperial family had passed to Dom Pedro Henrique who returned to Brazil in 1945. His descendants still hold the title but it is contested. Since 1987 monarchists have been trying to restore the monarchy through Congress but public support (as recorded in plebiscite) had fallen to 13 per cent by 1993. Congress has exploited divisions within the Imperial Family, as to who is the legitimate claimant, as the main reason for not proceeding with the issue.

Brunei

Short Title	HM Sultan Haji Hassanal Bolkiah of Brunei and Yang Di-Pertuan of Negara Darussalam
Born	15 July 1946, Brunei
Parents	HM Sultan Haji Omar Ali Saifuddien
Siblings	Prince Jefri
Religion	Muslim
Married	(not publicly available)
Consorts	HM Raja Isteri Pengiran Aanak Saleha HRH Pengiran Isteri Hajah Mariam
Children	4 sons, 6 daughters
Residence	Istana Nurul Iman Palace
Succeeded	1967
Status	Head of state and government
Income	Private

The Dynasty

References to the sultanate are found in Chinese annals from the 6th and 7th centuries onwards, and Marco Polo refers to trade between Brunei and China in the thirteenth century. It was visited by Magellan's expediton in the sixteenth century when it dominated all Borneo and many surrounding islands. Its power declined in the 19th century when it sought British protection. It recovered full independence under the present Sultan in 1984.

HM Sultan Haji Hassanal Bolkiah

Bulgaria

Short Title	HM King Simeon II
Born	16 June 1937, Sofia
Parents	HM King Boris III HM Queen Joanna (née HRH Princess Joanna of Savoy)
Siblings	HRH Princess Marie Louise (Mrs Marie Louise Chrobok)
Religion	Eastern Orthodox
Married	21 January 1962
Consort	HM Queen Margarita; (née Margarita Gomes-Acebo Cejuela)
Children	HRH Crown Prince Kardám, 2 December 1962 HRH Prince Kyril, 11 July 1964 HRH Prince Kubrat, 5 November 1965 HRH Prince Konstantin, 5 December 1967 HRH Princess Kalina, 19 January 1972
Residence	Madrid
Succeeded	29 August 1943
Status	Head of royal family
Income	Private

The Dynasty

The independent Principality of Bulgaria was proclaimed on 3 March 1878 and was ratified by the First Treaty of Berlin in June of the same year. The first prince was forced to abdicate but in July 1887 Prince Ferdinand of Saxe-Coburg and Gotha was proclaimed Prince. In October 1908 full independence from Turkey was declared and Prince Ferdinand became King (Czar) of Bulgaria. Following the Second World War his grandson King Simeon was forced to leave the country and now lives in Spain. Since the collapse of communism he has visited his country on several occasions.

For more information e-mail: simbul@mad.servicom.es

HM King Simeon II

Burma

Short Title	HRH Prince Shewbomin of Burma
Born	1942, Magwe near Bagan (capital of first Burmese Empire)
Parents	Hla'Maung Than-Shwe
Siblings	Tun'Myint Kyaw'Tint Maung'Win Myint'Myint Khin'Maung'Lay Khin'Ma'gyi
Religion	Buddhist
Married	Single
Consort	
Children	
Residence	London
Succeeded	Formally acknowledged 1991
Status	Uncrowned constitutional monarch (in exile)
Income	Private

The Dynasty

Prince Shewbomin is descended from the Bagan line of the Emperors of the first Burmese Empire, which was at its height during the 11th and 12th centuries. Civil war followed until the mid 18th century when Alompra of Ava once more re-united the country. The British captured Rangoon in 1826. In 1885 King Thibaw challenged the British and lost. He was deported and in 1886 Burma became a province of India. In 1937 it was detached and given some self-governing powers. The Japanese occupied the country in 1942 and were initially welcomed because they allowed a degree of self-government. The British re-occupied the country in 1945, granting it independence outside the Commonwealth under its King in 1948. In 1962 due to the political unrest Prince Shewbomin was forced to leave his country and lives in exile in London.

HRH Prince Shewbomin

Cambodia

Short Title	HM Preah Bat Samdech Preah Norodom Sihanouk Varman
Born	31st October 1922, Phnom Penh
Parents	HM King Norodom Suramarit HM Queen Sisowath Kossomak
Siblings	HRH Princess Norodom Vacheara, 17 August 1946 HRH Sdech Krom Khun Norodom Sirivudh, 8 June 1951 HRH Princes Norodom Preyasophon, 18 November 1954
Religion	Buddhist
Married	5 March 1955
Consort	HM Queen Norodom Monineath Sihanouk; (née Miss Monique Izzi)
Children	HRH Sdech Krom Khun Norodom Sihamoni HRH Prince Norodom Narindrapong
Residence	Khemarin Palace, Royal Palace, Phnom Penh
Succeeded	28 October 1941
Status	Head of state
Income	Private

The Dynasty

The dynasty can be traced back to the Angkor Empire, which was at its peak between the 9th and 14th centuries. By the 18th century the centre of political and economic activity had moved to Phnom Penh, the present capital. Cambodia was dominated by its neighbours when France turned it into a protectorate in 1863. Cambodia regained its independence in 1953 under the leadership of King Norodom Sihanouk Varman.
The King abdicated in 1955 and his parents became King and Queen. The monarchy was abolished in 1970 following a coup d'etat. It was re-established in September 1993 following a UN supervised election.

HM Preah Bat Samdech Preah Norodom Sihanouk Varman

Denmark

Short Title	HM Queen Margrethe II
Born	16 April 1940, Amalienborg Palace, Copenhagen
Parents	HM King Frederik IX HM Queen Ingrid (née Princess Ingrid of Sweden)
Siblings	HRH Princess Benedikte, 29 April 1944 HM Queen Anne-Marie of Greece, 30 August 1946
Religion	Evangelical Lutheran
Married	10 June 1967
Consort	HRH Prince Henrik; (né Henri-Marie-Jean-Andre, Count de Laborde de Monpezat)
Children	HRH Crown Prince Frederik, 26 May 1968 HRH Prince Joachim, 7 June 1969
Residence	Amalienborg Palace, Copenhagen
Succeeded	14 January 1972
Status	Head of state
Income	Private and state

The Dynasty

The Oldenburg family can trace its descent back more than a thousand years in an unbroken line of fifty-two monarchs to King Harald who established the kingdom. The three Scandinavian kingdoms were united by the Kalmar Union in 1397, but Sweden soon broke away. In 1450 Christian I was elected King of Norway and Norway remained united to Denmark till 1814 when it was ceded to Sweden. In 1849, during the reign of Frederick VII 1848-63, Denmark became a constitutional monarchy. Christian X (1912-47), worked to keep Denmark out of the conflict during the First World War and stayed in Denmark throughout the German occupation of the country during the Second World War. The present queen is only the second woman to occupy the throne.

HM Queen Margrethe II

Ethiopia

Short Title	HIH Crown Prince Zera Yacob Amha-Selassie
Born	1953, Addis Addaba
Parents	HIH Emperor Amha-Selassie (self proclaimed 1992)
Siblings	3 sisters
Religion	Orthodox Christian
Married	Previously married
Consort	
Children	HIH Princess Ledeta Zera Yacob
Residence	Manchester, England
Succeeded	1997
Status	A regency exists with HIH Prince Ermias Selassie who is President of the Crown Council and HIH Prince Bekere Fikre Selassie as the Viceroy. The Princes were appointed by the late Emperor Amha-Selassie and these appointments remain in effect to the present day.
Income	Private

The Dynasty

HIH Crown Prince Zera Yacob Amha-Selassie is a member of the House of Shoa (Solomonic dynasty) which has ruled Ethiopia since 1261. During the 16th century the state was threatened by Muslim invaders. Throughout the 18th and most of the 19th century the Kings were dominated by a number of provincial rulers. This situation changed in 1889 with the succession of Menyelek of Shoa who founded the modern state of Ethiopia. The rule of Haile Selassie, Emperor from 1930 to 1974, was interrupted in 1936 following an Italian invasion and conquest. He was restored by the British in 1941, to be deposed by republican revolutionaries in 1974. The Crown Prince lives in exile in Manchester, England. There is a Crown Council made up of members who are resident in Washington DC, which is the decision making-body of the Ethiopian Monarchy Movement.

HIH Prince Ermias Selassie

HIH Prince Bekere Fikre Selassie

France - The Royal House

Short Title	HRH Prince Henri, Comte de Paris
Born	14 June 1933, Manoir d'Anjou, nr Brussels
Parents	HRH Prince Henri, Comte de Paris HRH Princess Isabelle d'Orléans and Bragança
Siblings	HRH Princess Isabelle, 8 April 1932 (married Count Friedrich von Schönborn-Buchheim) HRH Princess Hélène, 17 September 1934 (married Count Evrard van Limburg-Stirum) HRH Prince François, 15 August 1935 (deceased) HRH Princess Anne, 4 December 1938 (married Prince Carlos de Bourbon) HRH Princess Diane, 24 March 1940 (married Duke Karl of Württemberg) HRH Prince Jacques, 25 June 1941 (married Gersende de Sabran-Pontevès) HRH Prince Michel, 25 June 1941 (married Béatrice Pasquier de Franclieu) HRH Princess Claude, 11 December 1943 (married Amédée of Savoy, Duke of Aosta) HRH Princess Chantal, 9 January 1946 (married Baron François-Xavier de Sambucy de Sorgue) HRH Prince Thibaut, 20 January 1948
Religion	Roman Catholic
Married	5 July 1957; 31 October 1984
Consort	1. HRH Princess Marie Thérèse (née Duchess Marie-Thérèse of Württemberg) 2. HRH Princess de Joinville (née Micaela San Carlos)
Children	HRH Princess Marie, 3 January1959 HRH Prince François, 7 February 1961 (Heir) HRH Princess Blanche, 10 September 1962 HRH Prince Jean, 19 May 1965 HRH Prince Eudes, 18 March 1968
Residence	Paris
Succeeded	19 June 1999
Status	Head of the royal house
Income	Private

HRH Prince Henri, Comte de Paris

The Dynasty

Henri d'Orléans, Comte de Paris, descends directly from Hugh Capet, 10th-century king of France. With the accession of Henri de Bourbon, King of Navarre, as Henry IV of France in 1589, the dynasty's name changed from Valois to Bourbon. The Bourbons ruled till 1789 and again from 1814 to 1848. After the collapse of the Second Empire in 1870 there was a move to restore the monarchy in the person of Henri V, the last surviving member of the senior Bourbon line, but he refused to accept the tricolour as his national flag and the attempt came to nothing.

The majority of the French legitimists now regard Louis-Philippe's great-grandson, Monseigneur Henri d'Orléans, Comte de Paris as the rightful pretender to the throne, last occupied by King Louis Philippe in 1848.

France - The Imperial House

Short Title	HIH Prince Charles Napoléon
Born	19 October 1950, Boulogne-sur-Seine
Parents	HIH Prince Louis Napoléon
	Alix de Foresta
Siblings	HIH Princess Catherine, 19 October 1950
	HIH Princess Laure, 8 October 1952
	HIH Prince Jérôme, 14 January 1957
Religion	Roman Catholic
Married	19 December 1978; 30 October 1996
Consort	1. Princess Béatrice of Bourbon-Two Sicilies
	2. Françoise Valliccioni
Children	HIH Princess Caroline, 24 October 1980
	HIH Prince Jean-Christophe, 11 July 1986
Residence	Villa de Prangins, Switzerland
Succeeded	3 May 1997
Status	Head of the imperial house
Income	Private

The Dynasty

The Buonopartes, the Italian spelling, were a noble Florentine family, a branch of which settled in 1512 in Corsica where Napoléon was born. He rose to prominence during the French Revolutionary Wars and proclaimed himself Emperor of the French in 1804. He set his several brothers on existing or created thrones in the parts of Europe then under French control. The head of the family until his death in May 1997 was Prince Louis Napoléon a descendant of Jérôme, King of Westphalia, Napoléon I's brother. After the Second World War (in which he had served with distinction) he lived in France unofficially until the 1886 law of exile was repealed, after which he openly maintained a house and secretariat in Paris. There is a Bonapartist Party in France, but the Prince was cautious not to allow its name to be used for party politics. His son and heir Prince Charles was married to a Bourbon princess, linking the Bonapartes with connections of the family of the traditional rulers of France.

HIH Prince Charles Napoléon

Germany - Bavaria

Short Title	HRH Duke Franz von Bayern
Born	14 July 1933, Munich
Parents	HRH Duke Albrecht von Bayern HRH Duchess Marita
Siblings	HRH Princess Marie Gabrielle, 30 May 1931 HRH Princess Marie Charlotte, 30 May 1931 HRH Prince Max Emanuel, 21 January 1937
Religion	Roman Catholic
Married	Single
Consort	
Children	
Residence	Munich
Succeeded	8 July 1996
Status	Head of the royal house of Bavaria
Income	Private

The Dynasty

The House of Wittelsbach has ruled Bavaria since 1180, when Otto V, Count Palatine, was invested with the Duchy. They became Electors in 1623. The first 19th century ruler, Maximilian, who succeeded as Elector in 1799, having allied himself to Napoleon, was rewarded with substantial additional territory and in 1805 the title of King. A change of sides when Napoleon's fortunes altered put the family in a strong position in 1815. Bavaria was incorporated into the German Empire in 1871, but with greater independence than other German states as a reward for supporting Wilhelm of Prussia as German Emperor. As in the rest of Germany, in 1918 the Bavarian Royal House ceased to rule. However, in 1921 they were restored to their estates and ancestral palaces. These were inherited by Duke Franz in 1996. The family continues to be popular.

HRH Duke Franz von Bayern

Germany - Hanover

Short Title	HRH Prince Ernst August V
Born	26 February 1954, Hanover
Parents	HRH Prince Ernst August IV
	HRH Princess Ortrud zu Schleswig-Holstein
Siblings	HRH Princess Marie Victoria, 1952
	HRH Prince Ludwig Rudolph, 1958
	HRH Princess Olga, 1958
	HRH Princess Alexandra, 1959
	HRH Prince Heinrich, 1961
Religion	Evangelical Lutheran
Married	28 August 1981, 23 January 1999
Consort	1.HRH Princess Chantal (née Hochuli)
	2.HSH Princess Caroline of Monaco
Children	HRH Ernst August, 19 July 1983
	HSH Prince Christian, 1 june 1985
Residence	Schulenburg an der Leine, Germany, and London
Succeeded	9 December 1987
Status	Prince of Hanover, Prince of Great Britain and Ireland, Duke of Brunswick & Lüneburg
Income	Private

The Dynasty

Emperor Frederick II created Otto I Duke of Brunswick in 1235. Otto added Hanover to his territories and all subsequent members of the family are descended from him. In 1692 Ernst August was created Elector of Hanover. His son, George Louis, through his mother succeeded to the throne of Great Britain in 1714 as George I and for over a century Hanover was ruled from Britain. At the end of the Napoleonic Wars Hanover became a kingdom with George III becoming its King. By the operation of Salic Law the two crowns were separated when Queen Victoria came to the throne and her uncle, the Duke of Cumberland, succeeded as Ernst August I. In 1866 Hanover was annexed to the German Empire and GeorgV deposed but left with the title of Prince of Hanover and Duke of Brunswick and Cumberland. Prince Ernst August II was deprived of his British dukedom in 1917. The family ceased to rule in 1918. The right to British nationality was established in 1956.

Germany - Prussia

Short Title	HIRH Prince Georg Friedrich, Prince of Prussia
Born	10 June 1976, Bremen
Parents	HIRH Prince Louis Ferdinand
	HIRH Princess Donata
Siblings	Princess Cornelia-Cécile, 30 January 1978
Religion	Evangelical Lutheran
Married	Single
Consort	
Children	
Residence	Lensahn, Ostholstein, Germany
Succeeded	25 September 1994
Status	Head of the imperial and royal house of Prussia
Income	Private

The Dynasty

The Hohenzollern dynasty can trace its rise in influence to the early 15th century when the Holy Roman Emperor Sigismund granted the Electorate of Brandenburg to the descendants of Count Thassilo, a 9th-century landowner with a castle on Zollern Hill in the Swabian Alps. By the 18th century the Electorate of Brandenburg had been transformed into the Kingdom of Prussia, and in its second half Frederick II, the Great, both by masterful government and military success, greatly increased the power of his country. In 1870 King Wilhelm I of Prussia accepted the invitation of King Ludwig II of Bavaria (instigated by Bismarck) to revive the German imperial title. He became Emperor of Germany in January 1871. The Empire survived until the defeat of Germany in 1918. After the flight of Kaiser Wilhelm II to Holland, the German Empire and all its constituent kingdoms, grand duchies and other states were abolished. Prince Georg Friedrich is the great-great-grandson of the last Kaiser.

Germany - Saxony

Short Title	HRH Prince Maria Emanuel, Margrave of Meissen
Born	31 January 1926, Prüfening
Parents	HRH Prince Friedrich, Markgraf zu Meissen HRH Princess Elisabeth von Thurn und Taxis
Siblings	HRH Princess Maria Josepha, 20 September 1928 HRH Princess Maria Anna, 13 December 1929 HRH Prince Albert, 30 November 1934 (heir) HRH Princess Mathilde, 17 January 1936
Religion	Roman Catholic
Married	23 June 1962
Consort	HRH Princess Anastasia-Luise (née Princess Anastasia-Luise of Anhalt)
Children	None
Residence	Switzerland
Succeeded	
Status	Head of the royal house of Saxony
Income	Private

The Dynasty

Originally a region of northwest Germany the ancient Duchy of Saxony broke up in 1180, but a portion of it, Wittenburg, was to form the basis of the later Saxony located in Eastern Germany. In 1423 the Emperor Sigismund gave the Electoral Duchy of Saxe-Wittenburg to Friedrich, Margrave of Meissen. Under Frederick the Wise (d.1525) Saxony became the most powerful state of the Empire and the cradle of the Reformation. In 1696 Augustus the Strong offered imself as King of Poland and preoccupation with that aspiration left Saxony at the mercy of warring armies for much of the 18th century. The Electorate became a kingdom in 1806 when Frederick Augustus III sided with Napoleon. The new kingdom survived his downfall but was increasingly drawn into the orbit of Prussia. It sided with Austria in 1866 and suffered as a consequence. In 1918 Saxony became a province of the German Republic. The present head of the family is childless and his brother Prince Albert is heir.

Germany - Württemberg

Short Title	HRH Prince Carl, Duke of Württemberg
Born	1 August 1936, Schloss Friedrichshafen, Württemberg
Parents	HRH Prince Phillipp, Duke of Württemberg HRH Archduchess Rosa of Austria
Siblings	HRH Duchess Marie Christine, 2 September 1924 HRH Duchess Helene, 29 June 1929 HRH Duke Ludwig, 23 October 1930 HRH Duchess Elisabeth, 2 February 1933 HRH Duchess Marie-Therese, 12 November 1934 HRH Duchess Marie-Antoinette, 31 August 1937
Religion	Roman Catholic
Married	18 July 1960
Consort	HRH Princess Diane (née Princess Diane d'Orleans)
Children	HRH Duke Friedrich, 1 June 1961 HRH Duchess Mathilde, 11 July 1962 HRH Duke Eberhard, 20 June 1963 HRH Duke Phillipp, 1 November 1964 HRH Duke Michael, 1 December 1965 HRH Duchess Eleanora, 4 November 1977
Residence	Schloss Altshausen and Schloss Friedrichshafen, Germany
Succeeded	15 April 1975
Status	Head of the royal house of Württemberg
Income	Private

The Dynasty

The family took their name from their ancient castle near Stuttgart in southwest Germany. In 1801 they ceded possessions to Napoleon in exchange for other territories and were given the title of Elector. In 1805 they sided with France and were rewarded with the title of king. King Frederick married as his second wife Princess Charlotte, a daughter of George III of Great Britain, which helped his standing with the Allies, enabling him to retain his royal title and most of his lands after the fall of Napoleon. Despite the agitations of 1848 and siding with Austria prior to German unification in 1866, the kingdom enjoyed peace till the First World War. It was abolished in 1918, but the lands were later restored.

Greece

Short Title	HM King Constantine II of the Hellenes
Born	2 June 1940, Psychiko, near Athens
Parents	HM King Paul HM Queen Frederika
Siblings	HM Queen Sophia of Spain HRH Princess Irene
Religion	Greek Orthodox
Married	18 September 1964
Consort	HM Queen Anne-Marie; (née Priness Anne Marie of Denmark)
Children	HRH Princess Alexia, 10 July 1965 HRH Crown Prince Pavlos, 20 May 1967 HRH Prince Nikolaos, 1 October 1969 HRH Princess Theodora, 9 June 1983 HRH Prince Philippos, 26 April 1986
Residence	London
Succeeded	6 March 1964
Status	Constitutional monarch in exile
Income	Private

The Dynasty

Greece became an independent Kingdom in 1830. The influential Greek aristocracy that had developed under Turkish rule agreed that unity amongst themselves could only be achieved with a monarch from outside their families. The first Greek monarch was Prince Otto of Bavaria, 1832-62, who was deposed and exiled after a military revolt. The next from whom the present royal family descends, was a Danish Prince, King George I of the Hellenes, 1863-1913. He was assassinated by a Turk. The next two monarchs, Constantine I, 1913-22 and George II, 1922-1947 were each deposed, exiled and recalled a total of five times. In 1947 George II was recalled after a referendum, but died shortly after his return. King Paul reigned from 1947 to 1964. Constantine II succeeded his father in 1964. He fled to Rome in 1967 after an abortive coup against the military government which had seized power earlier in the year. He was deposed in June 1973 and the monarchy was abolished by referendum in 1974.

HM King Constantine II of the Hellenes

Italy

Short Title	HRH Prince Vittorio Emanuele of Italy
Born	12 February 1937, Royal Palace Naples
Parents	HM King Umberto II HM Queen Marie José (née Princess Marie José of Belgium)
Siblings	HRH Princess Maria Pia, 24 September 1934 HRH Princess Maria Gabriella, 24 February 1940 HRH Princess Maria Beatrice, 2 February 1943
Religion	Roman Catholic
Married	7 October 1971
Consort	HRH Princess Marina (née Marina Doria)
Children	HRH Prince Emanuele Filiberto, 22 June 1972
Residence	Geneva, Switzerland
Succeeded	1971
Status	Legitimate claimant to the throne of Italy
Income	Private

The Dynasty

In the Middle Ages Savoy was a county of the Holy Roman Empire, today it is a region of France. The Savoy Family acquired extensive lands in north-western Italy and Piedmont throughout the 13th and 14th centuries, which were united with Savoy in the 15th century when their original lands became a duchy. In 1720 the Duke of Savoy obtained Sardinia, becoming its king. After the fall of Napoleon in 1815 their mainland possessions were restored and enlarged as the Kingdom of Sardinia. The Treaty of Villafranca in 1860 ceded Lombardy to Sardinia, but also ceded Savoy and Nice to France. In February 1861 Victor Emmanuel II, King of Sardinia, became the first King of Italy. Over the next nine years the other independent states of the Italian peninsula were unified as a constitutional monarchy. Victor Emmanuel III, who reigned from 1900 to 1946, supported Mussolini even though the role of King became a constitutional façade. He abdicated in 1946 in favour of his son Umberto II, who in turn abdicated one month later following a national referendum which declared in favour of a republic. In 1947 the

HRH Prince Vittorio Emanuele

family and their descendants were banned from Italy for ever, but members of the royal family may now be buried in Italy and female members may visit.

Japan

Short Title	HIM Emperor Akihito
Born	23 December 1933, Tokyo
Parents	HIM Emperor Hirohito (posthumously Emperor Showa) HIM Empress Nagako
Siblings	HIH Prince Hitachi HIH Princess Teru HIH Princess Taka HIH Princess Yori HIH Princess Suga
Religion	Shinto
Married	10 April 1959
Consort	HIM Empress Michiko; (née Michiko Shoda)
Children	HIH Crown Prince Naruhito, 23 February 1960 HIH Prince Akishino, 30 November 1965 HIH Princess Sayako, 18 April 1969
Residence	Imperial Palace, Tokyo
Succeeded	7 January 1989
Status	Head of state
Income	Private

The Dynasty

HM Emperor Akihito is directly related to Emperor Jimmu (fl.c. 40BC) However, it is only in recent times that the Emperor has held any political power, which had been usurped by the Shogun, hereditary commander-in-chief and virtual ruler. The Tokigawa Shogunate (1603-1867) was characterised by prosperity and isolationism. After 1867 the emperor was restored to power and Japan adopted Western institutions and technology. The constitution of 1947 excluded the emperor from executive power. Emperor Hirohito became regent for his father in 1921, succeeding as 'The Imperial Son of Heaven' in 1926. In 1946 he announced that he was not a god and renounced his divinity. In 1989 he was succeeded on the Chrysanthemum Throne by his son Emperor Akihito.

HIM Emperor Akihito

Jordan

Short Title	HM King Abdullah II bin Al Hussien
Born	30 January 1962, Amman
Parents	HM King Hussein bin Talal
	HRH Princess Muna (née Toni Gardiner)
Siblings	HRH Princess Alia, 13 February 1956
	HRH Prince Feisal, 11 October 1963
	HRH Princesses Zein and Aisha, 23 April 1968
	HRH Princess Haya, 3 May 1974
	HRH Prince Hamzah, 29 March 1980
	HRH Prince Hashem, 10 June 1981
	HRH Princess Iman, 24 April 1983
	HRH Princess Ralyah, 9 February 1986
	Adopted sister, Abir Muhaisin
Religion	Muslim
Married	10 June 1993
Consort	HM Queen Rania Al Abdullah
Children	HRH Prince Al Hussein, 28 June 1994
	HRH Princess Iman, 7 September 1996
Residence	Amman
Succeeded	7 February 1999
Status	Head of state
Income	Private and state

The Dynasty

King Abdullah II is a direct descendant in the 43rd generation of the Prophet Muhammad, through the male line of the Prophet's grandson, Al-Hassan. King Abdullah's branch of the Hashemite family ruled in Mecca from 1201 until 1925. His great-great-grandfather, Sharif Hussein bin Ali, Emir of Mecca, led the Great Arab Revolt of 1916 against the Turks. Sharif Hussein's second son, Abdullah, founded the Emirate of Transjordan in 1921. The Emirate assumed the name of the Hashemite Kingdom of Jordan upon formal independence from Britain in 1946.

HM King Abdullah II bin Al Hussien

When King Abdullah I was assassinated in 1951, his eldest son Talal ascended the throne. Because of the new King's poor health his eldest son Hussein was proclaimed king less than a year later. A Regency Council was appointed until he came of age. On 2 May 1953 he formally ascended the throne. He played a key role in Middle Eastern affairs during his long reign. He was succeeded by his eldest son.

Kuwait

Short Title	HH Amir Jabir Al Ahmad Al-Jabir Al-Sabah
Born	1928, Kuwait
Parents	Shaikh Ahmad Al-Sabah
Siblings	(not publicly available)
Religion	Muslim
Married	(not publicly available)
Consort	(not publicly available)
Children	(not publicly available)
Residence	Kuwait City
Succeeded	31 December 1977
Status	Head of state and government
Income	Private

The Dynasty

The Al-Sabah family have ruled in an unbroken line of thirteen rulers since 1756. The first Shaikh of Kuwait was Sabah I. From 1899 until 1961 the British provided military protection in return for an influence over Kuwait's relations with other states. During the First World War Shaikh Mubarak and his two sons, Tabir II and Salem fought against the Turks, allying themselves with the British. Kuwaiti oil resources were discovered before the Second World War but it was 1946 before production of oil was started. It was Shaikh Abd Allah III who first used oil wealth to develop his country in the 1950s; he is referred to as the architect of modern Kuwait The present ruler, Jabir III of Kuwait, now bears the title of Amir and is accorded the style of Highness.

HH Amir Jabir Al-Ahmad Al-Jabir Al-Sabah

Lesotho

Short Title	HM King Letsie III
Born	17 July 1963, Matseing
Parents	HM King Bereng Seeiso (Moshoeshoe II)
	HM Queen 'M'Amohato B. Seeiso
Siblings	HRH Seeiso B. Seeiso
	HRH 'M' Aseiso B. Seeiso
Religion	Roman Catholic
Married	Single
Consort	
Children	
Residence	The Royal Palace, Maseru
Succeeded	7 February 1996
Status	Head of state
Income	State

The Dynasty

Lesotho is a recently created kingdom in southern Africa completely surrounded by South Africa. It was formerly known as Basutoland and was created in response to Zulu conquests in the early 19th century. It was a British protectorate from 1884 until 1966 when it became an independent Kingdom within the Commonwealth. The Paramount Chief of Basutoland became its first King in 1966. He reigned as King Moshoeshoe II until his death in 1996 and was succeeded by his son Letsie.

HM King Letsie III

Libya

Short Title	HRH Prince Idris Abdallah Al Senussi
Born	18 January 1957, Benghazi
Parents	HRH Prince Abdallah Al Senussi
	HRH Princess Ghalia Nour Saleh
Siblings	HRH Prince Hashem, 6 September 1950
	HRH Princess Suzann, 25 April 1955
	HRH Princess Mahdi, 8 February 1956
	HRH Princess Salwa, 6 February 1963
	HRH Princess Suhalia, 9 August 1965
Religion	Muslim
Married	23 March 1987
Consort	HRH Princess Ana Maria; (née Ana Maria Quinones)
Children	HRH Princess Alia Al Senussi, 20 February 1983
	HRH Prince Khaled Al Senussi, 23 February 1988
Residence	London
Succeeded	March 1989
Status	Heir Apparent
Income	Private

The Dynasty

Idris Al Senussi, who had been elected as the most suitable ruler by the
Al Senussi Brotherhood, reigned from 1951 to 1969, and is the only
monarch to have ruled Libya. He was the leader of the Senussi tribesmen.
The tribe's principal objective in the 20th century was the removal of
foreign occupation forces, first the Turks, then the Italians and finally the
military administration of the Allied Powers. Libya was an independent
constitutional monarchy under King Idris, when, in 1969, a coup lead by
Colonel al-Qadhafi imposed a socialist republic. The Libyan
monarchical movement aims to restore a democratically elected
government to Libya with the king as a constitutional monarch.
Prince Idris Al Senussi is the claimant to the Libyan throne.

HRH Prince Idris Abdallah Al Senussi

Liechtenstein

Short Title	HSH Prince Hans-Adam II
Born	14 February 1945, Zurich
Parents	HSH Prince Franz Joseph II HSH Princess Gina
Siblings	Prince Philip, 19 August 1946 Prince Nicklas, 24 October 1947 Princess Nora, 31 October 1950 Prince Wenzel, 9 November 1962
Religion	Roman Catholic
Married	30 July 1967
Consort	HSH Princess Marie; (née Countess Marie Kinsky von Wchinitz und Tettau)
Children	Prince Alois, 11 June 1968 Prince Maximilian, 16 May 1969 Prince Constantin, 15 March 1972 Princess Tatjana, 10 April 1973
Residence	Vaduz Castle
Succeeded	13 November 1989
Status	Head of state
Income	Private and state

The Dynasty

Prince Johann Adam of Liechtenstein bought two fiefs of the Holy Roman Empire, the lordships of Verduz and Schellenburg in 1699 and 1712. His cousin Anton Florian, who succeeded him, was recognised as sovereign by the Emperor Charles VI in 1719, when these lands were erected into the Principality of Liechtenstein. No sovereign of Liechtenstein visited the Principality before 1842. During the 70-year reign of Johann II, 1858-1928, the people of the principality and the ruling family were brought closer together. The family's ties to the principality were further strengthened when their lands in Bohemia (now the Czech Republic) were lost to them during the late 1930s. Prince Hans-Adam II, the reigning Prince of Liechtenstein, remains the only sovereign in the German speaking world and, indeed, in the whole of Central Europe.

HSH Prince Hans-Adam II

Luxembourg

Short Title	HRH Grand Duke Jean of Luxembourg, Duke of Nassau, Prince of Bourbon-Parma
Born	5 January 1921, Château de Colmar-Berg
Parents	HRH Grand Duchess Charlotte HRH Prince Felix of Bourbon-Parma
Siblings	HRH Elizabeth, 22 December 1922 HRH Marie Adelaide, 21 May 1924 HRH Marie Gabrielle, 10 August 1925 HRH Charles, 7 August 1927 HRH Alix, 24 August 1929
Religion	Roman Catholic
Married	9 April 1953
Consort	HRH Grand Duchess Josephine-Charlotte; (née HRH Princess Josephine-Charlotte of Belgium)
Children	HRH Princess Marie-Astrid, 17 February 1954 HRH Prince Henri, 6 April 1955? (Heir) HRH Prince Jean, 15 May 1957 HRH Princess Marguerite, 15 May 1957 HRH Prince Guillaume, 1 May 1963
Residence	Château de Colmar-Berg
Succeeded	12 November 1964 on the abdication of his mother HRH Grand Duchess Charlotte
Status	Head of state
Income	State

The Dynasty

The Grand Duchy of Luxembourg has been ruled by the Dukes of Nassau since 1890 when they inherited it from their cousins, the Orange-Nassau dynasty of the Netherlands. When Nassau was annexed by Prussia in 1866, Duke Adolphe went into exile. He was 73 when he became reigning sovereign of Luxembourg, ruling until his death in 1905 at the age of 88. The Grand Ducal throne passed to his son, grand-daughter and in 1964 to the present Grand Duke Jean, who succeeded on the abdication of his mother.

HRH Grand Duke Jean of Luxembourg

Malaysia

Short Title	HM Yang di-Pertuan Agong (King) Sultan Salahuddin Abdul Aziz Shah
Born	8 March 1926, Bandar Temasha, Kuala Langat
Parents	HRH Sultan Hishamuddin Alam Shah, 7th Sultan of Selangor
Siblings	
Religion	Muslim
Married	1990
Consort	HM Raja Permaisuri Agong (Queen) (née Cik Puan Besar Selangor Siti Aishah)
Children	10 sons, 4 daughters
Residence	Istana Negara (Royal Palace), Kuala Lumpur
Succeeded	26th April 1999
Status	Head of state
Income	Private and state

The Dynasty

By the end of the 15th century most of peninsular Malaya was ruled by the Sultanate of Malacca which declined when the port of Malacca fell to the Portuguese in 1511. Other Sultanates were established under branches of its ruling dynasty in the following centuries. The Malay peninsula came under British control during the course of the 19th century, but regained its independence in 1957 as the main component of the state of Malasia. The modern federal state consists of the peninsula and territories of Sabah and Sarawak in North Borneo. There is an elective monarchy, the rulers of the states comprising the federation elect one of their number as monarch of the federation for a five year term. The present king the Sultan of Selangor is the 11th holder of the office.

HM Yang di-Pertuan Agong
Sultan Salahuddin Abdul Aziz Shah

Monaco

Short Title	HSH Prince Rainier III, The Sovereign Prince of Monaco
Born	31 May 1923, Monaco
Parents	HSH Princess Charlotte Prince Pierre (né Comte Pierre de Polignac)
Siblings	HSH Princess Antoinette, 20 December 1920
Religion	Roman Catholic
Married	18 April 1956
Consort	Princess Grace-Patricia, (née Grace Patricia Kelly)
Children	HSH Princess Caroline, 23 January 1957 HSH Hereditary Prince Albert, 14 March 1958 HSH Princess Stephanie, 1 February 1965
Residence	Palais Princier, Monaco
Succeeded	9 May 1949
Status	Head of state and government
Income	Private and state

The Dynasty

The Grimaldi family have been lords of Monaco since 968. In 1641 France offered Monaco its protection and Prince Honoré II was created a peer of France. His grandson and successor, Louis I, was recognised as Prince of Monaco and accorded rank and prerogatives at the French Court. Until 1817 Monaco remained under the protection of France. During the French Revolution the family faced arrest and one relative went to the guillotine. Throughout the rule of Napoléon they fared better, and the future Honoré V was appointed as Grand Equerry to the Empress Joséphine. By the Treaty of Paris in 1814 the Prince of Monaco was reinstated in his principality. The present Prince, Rainier III, who has reigned since 1949, married the actress Grace Kelly in 1956. The heir to the Principality is their son Prince Albert, born in 1958.

HSH Prince Rainier III of Monaco

Morocco

Short Title	HM King Hassan II
Born	9 July 1929, Rabat
Parents	HM King Mohammed V
Siblings	HRH Prince Moulay Abdellah
	HRH Princess Lalla Nesha
	HRH Princess Lalla Aicha
	HRH Princess Lalla Amina
	HRH Princess Lalla Fatima Zaha
Religion	Muslim
Married	(not publicly available)
Consort	(not publicly available)
Children	HRH Princess Lalla Meriem, 26 August 1962
	HRH Crown Prince Sidi Mohammed, 21 August 1963
	HRH Princess Lalla Asma, 29 September 1965
	HRH Princess Lalla Housna, 19 November 1967
	HRH Prince Moulay Rachid, 20 June 1970
Residence	Rabat
Succeeded	3 March 1961
Status	Head of state
Income	Private and state

The Dynasty

Morocco has been ruled by the Filali dynasty since the 18th century. When the country became a French protectorate in 1912 the Sultan remained Sharif. In 1956 Morocco was proclaimed an independent sovereign state and the following year the Sultan assumed the title of King Mohammed V of Morocco. His son, Prince Moulay Hassan, succeeded him as King Hassan II in 1961. He is a direct descendant, in the 35th generation, of the prophet Mohammed.

King Hassan died on 23 July 1999 and was succeeded by his son Mohammed VI.

HM King Hassan II

Nepal

Short Title	HM King Birendra Bir Bikram Shah Dev
Born	28 December 1945
Parents	HM King Mahendra
	HRH Crown Princess Indra Rajya Laxmi Devi Shah
Siblings	2 brothers, 3 sisters
Religion	Hindu
Married	February 1970
Consort	HM Queen Aishwarya Rajya Laxmi Devi Shah
Children	HRH Crown Prince Dipendra Bir Bikram Shah Dev
	HRH Princess Sruti Rajya Laxmi Devi Rana
	HRH Prince Nirajam Bir Bikram Shah
Residence	Narayanhity Royal Palace, Nepal
Succeeded	31 January 1972
Status	Head of state
Income	Private and state

The Dynasty

The present dynasty derives from King Prithui Narayan Shah who conquered the present state of Nepal in 1769. The present monarch King Birendra Bir Bikram Shah Dev has reigned since 1972.

HM King Birendra Bir Bikram Shah Dev

The Netherlands

Short Title	HM Queen Beatrix
Born	31 January 1938, Soestdijk Palace, Baarn
Parents	HM Queen Juliana HRH Prince Bernhard
Siblings	HRH Princess Irene, 5 August 1939 HRH Princess Margriet, 19 January 1943 HRH Princess Christina, 18 February 1947
Religion	Dutch Reformed Church
Married	10 March 1966
Consort	HRH Claus, Prince of the Netherlands, (né Claus von Amsberg)
Children	HRH Crown Prince Willem-Alexander, Prince of Orange, 27 April 1967 HRH Prince Friso, 25 September 1968 HRH Prince Constantijn, 11 October 1969
Residence	Huis ten Bosch, The Hague
Succeeded	30 April 1980 (on the abdication of her mother)
Status	Head of state
Income	Private and state

The Dynasty

Queen Beatrix also bears the title Princess of Orange-Nassau.
Her family's links with the Netherlands go back to 1403 when Count
Engelbert I of Nassau in Germany married a Dutch heiress. A century and
a half later a descendant, William the Silent, Count of Nassau, inherited
from a cousin the Principality of Orange in France and that family's
estates in Holland. William the Silent led a successful rising against
Philip II of Spain and secured the independence of the northern
Netherlands. The Kingdom of the Netherlands was created in 1814 by the
union of Holland, Belgium and the Grand Duchy of Luxembourg;
however, Belgium proclaimed independence in 1830 (recognised by the
Dutch in 1839) and the Grand Duchy of Luxembourg became
independent in 1890. Queen Beatrix ascended the throne on the
abdication of her mother in 1980. The heir to the throne is Prince Willem-
Alexander. He is the first male heir in over a century.

HM Queen Beatrix

Norway

Short Title	HM Harald V
Born	21 February 1937, Skaugum, Oslo
Parents	HM Olav V
	HRH Crown Princess Märtha (née Princess Märtha of Sweden
Siblings	HRH Princess Ragnhild
	HRH Princess Astrid
Religion	Lutheran
Married	29 August 1968
Consort	HM Queen Sonja (née Sonja Haraldsen)
Children	HRH Princess Martha Louise, 22 September 1971
	HRH Crown Prince Haakon, 20 July 1973
Residence	Royal Palace, Oslo
Succeeded	17 January 1991
Status	Head of state
Income	Private and state

The Dynasty

Norway became an independent kingdom for the first time in nearly five centuries following the dissolution of the union with Sweden in 1905. Prince Carl of Denmark was elected King of Norway as Haakon VII, 1905-57, enjoying a long and popular reign. His only child succeeded to the throne on his death, as King Olav V, 1957-91. The current monarch is King Harald V who continues the Scandinavian tradition as a 'people's king'.

HM Harald V

Oman

Short Title	HM Sultan Qaboos bin Said Al-Said
Born	Oman
Parents	HM Sultan bin Tai Mour Al-Said
Siblings	(not publicly available)
Religion	Muslim
Married	Single
Consort	(not publicly available)
Children	(not publicly available)
Residence	Muscat, Oman
Succeeded	July 1970
Status	Head of state and government
Income	Private

The Dynasty

Sultan Qaboos bin Said al Said is the eighth ruler of the Al Busaidi dynasty which was founded in 1744 by Imam Ahmad bin Said.
He ascended the throne on the abdication of his father Sultan Said bin Taimur in July 1970. Since 1970 the Sultan has taken a leading role in advancing every aspect of his country's development. Three decades ago the country had suffered from over a century of stagnation with an accompanying lack of development, illiteracy, a high mortality rate and isolation. Since ascending the throne the Sultan has worked with his people to provide the health care, education and social requirements they need. Extensive oil revenues have funded the development of a modern and vibrant state.

HM Sultan Qaboos bin Said Al-Said

Portugal

Short Title	HRH Dom Duarte Duke of Bragança
Born	15 May 1945, Berne, Switzerland
Parents	HRH Dom Duarte, Infante of Portugal, Duke of Bragança
	HRH Maria Francisca d'Orléans e Bragança
Siblings	HRH Infante Dom Miguel, 3 December 1946
	HRH Infante Dom Henrique, 6 November 1949
Religion	Roman Catholic
Married	13 May 1995
Consort	HRH Dona Isabel Ines de Heredia
Children	HRH Infante Dom Afonso, Prince of Beira, 25 March 1996
	HRH Infanta Dona Maria Francisca, 3 March 1997
Residence	Lisbon
Succeeded	24 December 1976
Status	Head of the royal family
Income	Private and state

The Dynasty

The Aviz dynasty ruled Portugal from 1388-1580, acquiring vast overseas possessions in the 16th century, including Brazil of which they became emperors. The House of Bragança gave Portugal its monarchs from 1640 -1910, after John IV, Duke of Bragança, a descendant of the Aviz family, recovered Portugal's independence from Spain through rebellion. Manuel II was the last reigning monarch, succeeding his father, Carlos I, after his assassination in 1908. Manuel II abdicated in October 1910, and moved to London where he died without issue in 1932. He was succeeded by his cousin Dom Duarte whose right was impeccable but whose family had lived outside Portugal since 1834. However, Dom Duarte was able to return to Porugal in 1950 and was provided with a government allowance. He died in 1976 and was succeeded by his son, also Dom Duarte, born in 1945 and who continues to live in Portugal with his wife and children.

HRH Dom Duarte Duke of Bragança

Qatar

Short Title	HH Sheikh Hamad Bin Khalifa Al Thani
Born	1950, Doha
Parents	HH Sheikh Khalifa Bin Hamad Al Thani
Siblings	(not publicly available)
Religion	Muslim
Married	(not publicly available)
Consort	(not publicly available)
Children	(not publicly available)
Residence	Doha
Succeeded	27 June 1995
Status	Amir of the State of Qatar
Income	Private

The Dynasty

The Al-Thani family settled in the area of the Qatar peninsula in the early 18th century, becoming its rulers in the mid 19th century. The first Sheikh was Mohammed Bin Thani. The present Amir, Sheikh Hamad Bin Khalifa Al Thani, is the eighth member of his family to rule the state. He assumed the title in 1995 on the death of his father.

HH Sheikh Hamad Bin Khalifa Al Thani

Romania

Short Title	HM King Michael I
Born	25 October 1921, Foisor
Parents	HM King Carol II HRH Princess Helen of Greece
Siblings	HRH Prince Carol Mircea (half brother)
Religion	Romanian Orthodox
Married	10 June 1948
Consort	HM Queen Anne Antoinette (née HRH Princess Anne Antoinette of Bourbon-Parma)
Children	HRH Crown Princess Margarita, 26 March 1949 HRH Princess Helen, 15 November 1950 HRH Princess Inna, 28 February 1953 HRH Princess Sophie, 29 October 1957 HRH Princess Maria, 13 July 1964
Residence	Bern, Switzerland
Succeeded	1927-1930 and again 1940-47
Status	Constitutional monarch in exile
Income	Private

The Dynasty

In the mid-19th century the two Romanian principalities of Wallachia and Moldavia achieved self government from Turkey. They were united as the state of Romania in 1866 when they chose a member of the Hohenzollern dynasty as their Prince. In 1881 Prince Carol gained the independence of Romania from Turkey, and took the title King Carol. He was succeeded by his nephew Ferdinand in 1914. King Ferdinand's eldest son, Carol, (later King Carol II) married twice. His first marriage to Ioana Valentina Lambrino in August 1918 was annulled and in March 1921 he married Princess Helen of Greece. In 1927 their son Michael, as a minor, succeeded to the throne on the death of King Ferdinand, because Carol had renounced his rights of succession in 1925. He was, however, restored to his rights and proclaimed king as Carol II in 1930. He reigned until deposed by Hitler in 1940, when his son was reinstated as King Michael I until he in turn was forced to abdicate in 1947. Having no male heir, in 1997 King Michael announced a change in the dynastic law which will allow his oldest daughter to succeed him.

HM King Michael I

Russia

Short Title	HIH Grand Duke George Mikhailovich
Born	13 March 1981, Madrid, Spain
Parents	HIH Grand Duchess Maria Vladimirovna
	Grand Duke Michael (né HRH Prince Franz Wilhelm
	of Prussia)
Siblings	None
Religion	Russian Orthdox
Married	Single
Consort	
Children	
Residence	Madrid, Spain
Succeeded	1992
Status	Claimant to Russian throne
Income	Private

The Dynasty

The Romanov dynasty was the reigning family of Russia from 1613 to 1917. The last Tsar, Nicholas II, was murdered in 1918 at Ekaterinburg with his family. In 1924 HIH Grand Duke Kyril Vladimirovich was proclaimed Tsar in exile. Today his great-grandson Grand Duke George Mikhailovich is the claimant to the throne through his mother. He was born in 1981 and lives in Madrid, but is being educated in England. Due to his age, his mother, the Grand Duchess Maria, takes care of his interests at present. The head of the Romanov family through the male line is Prince Nicholas.

HIH Grand Duke George Mikhailovich

Rwanda

Short Title	HM King Kıgeli V
Born	29 June 1936, Kamembe, Shangugu Territory
Parents	HM King Musinga
	Mukashema
Siblings	HM King Mutara (deceased)
Religion	Roman Catholic
Married	Single
Consort	
Children	
Residence	Washington DC, USA
Succeeded	27 July 1959 upon the death of his brother HM King Mutara
Status	Constitutional monarch in political asylum
Income	Private

The Dynasty

The monarchy in Rwanda was instituted by the Belgians during the colonial era. The present monarch, Jean-Baptiste Ndahindurwa King Kigeli V ascended the throne on the death of his brother in 1959. During 1940 his father, King Yuhi Musinga, and his family were exiled by the Belgians. Jean-Baptiste Ndahindurwa returned to Rwanda first for his education (1944-51) and then to work with the Belgian administration (1956-9). Two years after his accession he was prevented by the Belgian government from returning to his country after a visit to Zaire to meet the Secretary General of the United Nations, and he has remained in exile since Rwanda's independence in 1962. Throughout the 1990s he has assisted refugees from Rwanda and kept the international community informed about events in his country.

HM King Kigeli V

Saudi Arabia

Short Title	HM King Fahd Bin Abdulaziz
Born	1920, Riyadh
Parents	HM King Abdulaziz Ibn Saud
	HM Queen Hussah Al-Sudairy
Siblings	HRH Prince Sultan
	HRH Prince Abdul Rahman
	HRH Prince Turki
	HRH Prince Naif
	HRH Prince Salman
	HRH Prince Ahmad
Religion	Muslim
Married	(not publicly available)
Consort	(not publicly available)
Children	HRH Prince Fasisal
	HRH Prince Mohammed
	HRH Prince Saud
	HRH Prince Sultan
	HRH Prince Khaled
	HRH Prince Abdulaziz
Residence	Royal Palace, Riyadh
Succeeded	13 June 1982
Status	Head of state and of government
Income	Private

The Dynasty

Al-Sa'ud is the ruling family of Saudi Arabia. The Kingdom was established by Abdul-Aziz Al-Sa'ud, Amir of Najd in 1932, after he had conquered the Al Rashid lands and the Hashimid kingdom of the Hijaz in the 1920s. The present Sa'udi kingdom has been ruled by King Fahd since 1982. The wealth of the country and its royal family comes from the exploitation of its vast oil reserves.

HM King Fahd Bin Abdulaziz

Spain

Short Title	HM King Juan Carlos
Born	5 January 1938, Rome
Parents	HRH Don Juan, Count of Barcelona, Prince of the Asturias
	HRH Dona María de las Mercedes of Bourbon-Two Sicilies
Siblings	HRH Infanta Maria del Pilar, 30 July 1936
	HRH Infanta Margarita, 6 March 1939
	HRH Infante Alfonso, 1941-56
Religion	Roman Catholic
Married	14 May 1962
Consort	HM Queen Sofia (née HRH Princess Sofia of Greece)
Children	HRH Infanta Elena, 20 December 1963
	HRH Infanta Cristina, 13 June 1965
	HRH Infante Felipe, Prince of the Asturias (Heir), 30 January 1968
Residence	Palacio de la Zarzuela, Madrid
Succeeded	22 November 1975
Status	Head of state
Income	Private and state

The Dynasty

The Bourbons succeeded the Habsburgs as the royal house of Spain when Philip, grandson of Louis XIV of France and great-grandson of Philip IV of Spain, inherited the throne in 1700. In 1808 Charles IV abdicated and Napoleon's brother Joseph became King. At the conclusion of the Peninsular War in 1813 Ferdinand VII reclaimed his family's throne. In 1931 King Alfonso XIII went into voluntary exile when Spain became a republic. In 1940 he abdicated in favour of his son Don Juan, who in turn ceded his rights to his son Juan Carlos who ascended the throne in 1975 when the monarchy was restored after the death of General Franco.

HM King Juan Carlos

Swaziland

Short Title	HM King Mswati III
Born	19 April 1968, Manzini
Parents	King Sobhuza II
	Ntombi Latfwala
Siblings	68 brothers
Religion	Traditional
Married	
Consort	Several wives
Children	Numerous
Residence	Ludzidzini
Succeeded	25 April 1986
Status	Head of state
Income	Private

The Dynasty

Swaziland is a modern kingdom in southern Africa. The state was founded in the early 19th century at the time of the Zulu conquests. It came under British protection at the end of the 19th century and continued with this status until 1967. During this time the King of the Swazis was recognised only as Paramount Chief. In 1968 it became an independent kingdom within the Commonwealth under King Sobhuza II of the House of Nkosi-Dlamini whose lineage can be traced back to the mid 18th century and King Ngwane III.

HM King Mswati III

Sweden

Short Title	HM King Carl XVI Gustaf
Born	30 April 1946, Stockholm
Parents	Crown Prince Gustaf Adolf Princess Sibylla of Saxe-Coburg-Gotha
Siblings	HRH Princess Margaretha (Mrs John Ambler), 31 October 1934 HRH Princess Birgitta (Princess Johan-George von Hohenzollen), 19 January 1937 HRH Princess Désirée (Baroness Silfverschiöld), 2 June 1938 HRH Princess Christina (Mrs. Tord Magnuson), 3 August 1943
Religion	Lutheran
Married	19 June 1976
Consort	HM Queen Silvia (née Silvia Renate Sommerlath)
Children	HRH Crown Princess Victoria, 14 July 1977 HRH Prince Carl Philip, 13 May 1979 HRH Princess Madeleine, 10 June 1982
Residence	Drottningholm, Stockholm
Succeeded	15 September 1973
Status	Head of state
Income	Private and state

The Dynasty

In 1810 one of Napoleon's Marshals was elected by the Swedish Estates as their Crown Prince. Marshal Jean Baptiste Bernadotte was Regent of the Realm from 1810 and, on the death of Karl XIII in 1818, he became King Karl XIV Johan. His successors married into the Orange-Nassau and British royal families. King Gustav V, 1907-50 kept Sweden neutral through two World Wars. His son King Gustav VI Adolph, 1950-73, was succeeded by his grandson in 1973. King Carl XVI Gustav, has proved to be a popular monarch with the support of his wife, Queen Silvia. The 1980 Act of Succession laid down that the eldest child, regardless of sex, would inherit the throne.

HM King Carl XVI Gustaf

Thailand

Short Title	IIM King Bhumibol Adulyadej (Rama IX)
Born	5 December 1927, Cambridge, Massachusetts, USA
Parents	HRH Prince Mahidol of Songkhla HRH Somdej Phra Sri Nakarindra Boromarajjonmani
Siblings	HRH Princess Galyani Wattana HM King Ananda Mahidol (Rama VIII)
Religion	Buddhist
Married	28 April 1950
Consort	HM Queen Sirikit; (née Mom Rajawongse Sirikit Kittiyakara)
Children	HRH Princess Ubol Ratana, 5 April 1951 HRH Crown Prince Mah Vajiralongkorn, 28 July 1952 HRH Princess Maha Chakri Sirindhorn, 2 April 1955 HRH Princess Chulabhorn, 4 July 1957
Residence	Chitralada Villa, Dusit Palace, Bangkok
Succeeded	9 June 1946 (on the death of his brother)
Status	Head of state
Income	Private

The Dynasty

The Royal House of Chakri was founded in 1782, at the same time as Bangkok was established as the capital. The present monarch King Bhumibol Adulyadej, born in Cambridge, Massachusetts, ascended the throne in 1946, at the age of 19, on the death of his brother. He is often referred to as the 'Farmer King' as agriculture and water supply are his particular interests. His only son Crown Prince Maha Vajiralongkorn is heir apparent.

HM King Bhumibol Adulyadej (Rama IX)

Tonga

Short Title	HM King Taufa'ahau Tupou IV
Born	4 July 1918, Nuku'alofa
Parents	HM Queen Salote Tupou III
	HRH Prince Tungi Mailefihi
Siblings	HRH Prince Fatafehi Tu'ipelehake
Religion	Christian
Married	10 June 1947
Consort	HM Queen Mata'aho
Children	HRH Crown Prince Tupouto'a
	HRH Princess Salote Mafilc'o Pilolevu Tuita
	HRH Prince 'Alaivahamama'o
	HRH Prince Lavaka-Ata-'Ulukalala
Residence	Royal Palace, Nuku'alofa
Succeeded	16 December 1965
Status	Head of state
Income	Private and state

The Dynasty

Three ancient Polynesian kingly lines were united in the mid-19th century by King Siaosi Tupou I. This dynasty still reigns and King Taufa'ahau Tupou IV is the current monarch.

King Taufa'ahau Tupou IV

Uganda - Buganda

Short Title	IIM Kabaka Rodney Muwenda Mutebi II
Born	13 April 1955, Kampala
Parents	HM Sir Edward Mutesa II
	Lady Sarah Kisosonkole
Siblings	Seven brothers and nine sisters
Religion	Protestant
Married	Single
Consort	
Children	
Residence	The Royal Palace, Kampala
Succeeded	31 July 1993
Status	Constitutional monarch
Income	Private

The Dynasty

The kingdom of Buganda had been firmly established by the seventeenth century and had become the dominant country in East Africa by the eighteenth century. When Uganda became an independent state in 1963 Mutesa II, 35th Kabaka of Buganda, became the first president of Uganda. He was deposed in 1966 and died in exile in London in 1969. He was succeeded by his son Mutebi who lived in exile in England until returning to Uganda in 1987. He was crowned 36th Kabaka of Buganda in 1993.

HM Kabaka Rodney Muwenda Mutebi II

Uganda - Bunyoro-Kitara

Short Title	HM King Solomon Gafabusa Iguru
Born	18 June 1949, Bunyoro
Parents	HM King Kito Winyi
Siblings	18 brothers and 54 sisters
Religion	Protestant
Married	Single
Consort	
Children	
Residence	The Royal Palace, Hoima District, Bunyoro
Succeeded	1993
Status	Constitutional monarch
Income	Private and state

The Dynasty

The kingdom of Bunyoro-Kitara in northwest Uganda is over a thousand years old. King Solomon, the 27th King in the Ababiita dynasty, was restored to the throne in June 1994.

HM King Solomon Gafabusa Iguru

Uganda - Toro

Short Title	HM King Oyo Nyimba Kabambaiguru Rukidi IV
Born	16 April 1992, Kampala
Parents	HM King David Matthew Patrick Olimi Kaboyo II
	HM Queen Best Kemigisi Olimi Akiiki
Siblings	Princess Nsemere Komuntale, 22 February 1989
	Princess Celia Komukyeya, 12 October 1993
Religion	Protestant
Married	Single
Consort	
Children	
Residence	Kabarole Palace, Fort-Portal, Toro
Succeeded	12 September 1995
Status	Regency as the king is a minor
Income	Private and state

The Dynasty

His Majesty King Oyo Nyimba Kabambaiguuru Rukidi IV ascended the throne after the death of his father in 1995. He is the 12th King of the Kingdom of Toro.

94

HM King Oyo Nyimba Kabambaiguru Rukidi IV

United Arab Emirates

Short Title	President: HH Sheikh Zayed bin Sultan Al'Nahyan
Born	*ca* 1915, Al' Ain's Jahili Fortress
Parents	HH Shaikh Sultan bin Zayed HH Shaikha Salama bint Bhutti
Siblings	HH Shaikh Shakbut (Ruler from 1928 - 1966)
Religion	Muslim
Married	(not publicly available)
Consort	HH Shaikha Fatima bint Mubarak; (née Fatima bint Mubarak)
Children	Khalifa (first Prime Minister of Abu Dhabi) Sultan Mohammad
Residence	Abu-Dhabi
Succeeded	6 August 1966
Status	Head of ruling family
Income	Private

The Dynasty

The United Arab Emirates (UAE) is a group of seven Arab Shaikhdoms (the Trucial States) who agreed to work together in the early 1970s. They formed the union after 150 years of British tutelage. Each of the seven states has its own royal household. Shaikh Zayed bin Sultan al-Nahyan is not only the ruler of Abu Dhabi, one of the seven shaikhdoms, but was elected President of the UAE in 1971 and re-elected a further four times. His family - the House of Al Bu Falah - has ruled Abu Dhabi since 1761. The Vice President of the UAE is HH Shaikh Maktoum bin Rashid al Maktoum, the ruler of Dubai. His family, the House of Al Bu Falasah has ruled Dubai since it gained independence from Abu Dhabi in 1833. Sharjah has been ruled by HH Shaikh Sultan bin Mohammad al-Qasimi of the House of Qasimi since 1972. Ras al-Khaimah has been governed by HH Shaikh Saqr bin Mohammad al-Qasimi since his uncle was deposed in 1948. In Ajman, the death of HH Shaikh Humaid bin Rashid al-Nu'aimi's father in 1981 led to his succession. Umm al-Qaiwain has been ruled by the Al-Ali family since the late 18th century.

President: HH Sheikh Zayed bin Sultan Al'Nahyan

Shaikh Rashid bin Ahmad al-Mualla succeeded on the death of his father in 1981. Fujairah has been governed by HH Shaikh Hamad bin Mohammad al-Sharqi since his father died in 1974.

United Kingdom

Short Title	HM Queen Elizabeth II
Born	21 April 1926, 17 Bruton Street, London, W1
Parents	HRH Prince Albert Duke of York, (later King George VI) The Duchess of York (née Hon. Elizabeth Bowes-Lyons) (now HM Queen Elizabeth The Queen Mother)
Siblings	HRH Princess Margaret, 21 August 1930
Religion	Church of England
Married	20 November 1947
Consort	HRH The Prince Philip, Duke of Edinburgh; (né Philip Mountbatten)
Children	HRH Prince Charles, Prince of Wales, 14 November 1948 HRH Princess Anne, The Princess Royal, 15 August 1950 HRH Prince Andrew, Duke of York, 19 February 1960 HRH Prince Edward, 10 March 1964
Residence	Buckingham Palace, London
Succeeded	6 February 1952
Status	Head of state
Income	Private and state

The Dynasty

The House of Windsor, the present name of the royal family, dates from 1917 when the Queen's grandfather, King George V felt it necessary to change the family's name of Saxe-Coburg-Gotha which it owed to Prince Albert, Queen Victoria's husband. Queen Victoria was the last monarch of the House of Hanover. George V's eldest son, Edward VIII, succeeded to the throne in January 1936, but abdicated in December of the same year to marry Mrs Simpson. His brother, George VI, the father of the present monarch, stayed in London throughout the Second World War. Queen Elizabeth II has moved the monarchy forward to fit the changing circumstances of the late 20th century.

HM Queen Elizabeth II

Queen Elizabeth II is also Queen of another 15 countries: Antigua and Barbuda, Australia, The Bahamas, Barbados, Belize, Canada, Grenada, Jamaica, New Zealand, Papua New Guinea, St. Christopher and Nevis, St. Lucia, St. Vincent & The Grenadines, Solomon Islands, Tuvalu.

Yugoslavia

Short Title	HRH Crown Prince Alexander
Born	17 July 1945, London
Parents	HM King Peter II
	HM Queen Alexandra (née Princess Alexandra of Greece)
Siblings	None
Religion	Serbian Orthodox
Married	1 July 1972 and 21 September 1985
Consort	1. HRH Princess Maria da Gloria (née HRH Princess Maria da Gloria d'Orleans and Braganza
	2. HRH Princess Katherine (née Katharine Batis)
Children	HRH Prince Peter, 5 February 1980
	HRH Prince Philip, 15 January 1982
	HRH Prince Alexander, 15 January 1982
Residence	London
Succeeded	3 November 1970
Status	Crown Prince in exile
Income	Private

The Dynasty

The Karadjordjevic dynasty is nearly 200 years old. In 1804 a wealthy clan chief Djordje Petrovic, known to his followers as Karadjordje (Black George) led the Serbs in a successful uprising against the Ottoman Empire which controlled the Balkans. Karadjordje established a government in Belgrade and in 1811 was confirmed as ruler and the right of succession was vested in his family. In November 1945 the monarchy was abolished without a referendum and Yugoslavia entered four decades of communist rule. King Peter II never abdicated. Crown Prince Alexander is now the head of the family and lives in exile in London. He earns a living as a successful businessman.
For more information visit http:/www.suc.org/royal

HRH Crown Prince Alexander

Yugoslavia - Montenegro

Short Title	HRH Crown Prince Nikola
Born	24 July 1944, Paris
Parents	HM King Michael I
	HRH Princess Geneviève
Siblings	None
Religion	Orthodox
Married	27 November 1976
Consort	HRH Princess Francine (née Francine Navarro)
Children	HRH Princess Altinai, 27 October 1977
	HRH Prince Boris, Hereditary Prince Petrovic-Njegos of Montenegro, 21 January 1980
Residence	Paris
Succeeded	24 March 1986
Status	Head of the royal house
Income	Private

The Dynasty

Montenegro is a region of south-western Yugoslavia known in medieval times as Zeta. In 1516 its people elected a prince bishop to rule them and maintain their independence. At the beginning of the 18th century this office became hereditary in the Petrovic-Njegos family.The ecclesiastical duties were given up mid 19th century to enable Danilo I to marry and establish a lay dynasty. He was succeeded in 1860 by his nephew Nikola I who assumed the title of King in 1910, but he was driven into exile in 1918 when Montenegro was annexed to what was to become the kingdom of Yugoslavia. King Nikola I did not accept the annexation and maintained a government-in-exile until his death in 1921. He was succeeded by his grandson King Michael I, but in 1922 the union of Montenegro with Serbia was internationally recognised by a Conference of Ambassadors in Paris. Prince Nikola is his son.

Also from Shepheard-Walwyn

THE PRINCE AND THE PROFESSOR

A dialogue on the place of monarchy in the 21st century

L.L. Blake with illustrations by Barrington Barber

The prince and the professor discuss a number of issues: the nature of sovereignty; the pros and cons of a republic; Plato on freedom and democracy; the role of the press; the notion of contract underlying modern written constitutions contrasted with the medieval concept of status in the British constitution.

The professor acknowledges that change there must be to adapt to the 21st century, but warns that currently the danger is that changes are forced through by politicians with little appreciation of their effect. The monarch has a role above and beyond politics, to look to the future well-being of the nation and to warn of pitfals.

'The author should be applauded for raising the debate about the purpose of monarchy to an intelligent level.' FINANCIAL TIMES

ISBN 0 85683 165 4 128pp Bibliography **£7.95 pb**

SOVEREIGNTY: POWER BEYOND POLITICS

L.L. Blake

The issue of sovereignty lies at the heart of debate about moves for closer integration in Europe. The author, a barrister, examines what sovereignty is and where in a nation it resides.

'This is a thought-provoking study on the power beyond politics.'

CONTEMPORARY REVIEW

ISBN 085683 097 6 144pp Index **£9.95 hb**

LITTLE MOTHER OF RUSSIA

A Biography of the Empress Marie Feodorovna

Coryne Hall

Empress Marie (1847-1928) lived one of the most dramatic lives of any princes to sit on the Russian throne. Born Princess Dagmar of Denmark, she was betrothed to the Tsarevitch Nicholas, oldest son of Alexander II. It was a love match on both sides, but he died shortly before the wedding. She married his brother who succeeded as Alexander III in 1881 on the assisnation of his father. Her son was Nicholas II, the last Tsar.

She had a happy marriage and exercised a moderating influence on her autocratic husband, but all that she loved was destroyed before her eyes. Her husband died in his prime and two sons died young. During the First World War, her advice unheeded, Nicholas II took command of the army and she could only watch as the country she loved was governed by Empress Alexandra and Rasputin, with disastrous results. After a period of house arrest under the Bolsheviks, she escaped and was brought to England aboard a British warship. She returned to Denmark, where she remained paramount among the Romanovs until her death in 1928.

ISBN 0 85683 177 8 350pp b & w photos Index **£25 hb**

WITNESS OF A CENTURY

The Life and Times of Prince Arthur, Duke of Connaught

Noble Frankland

Prince Arthur (1850-1942) was Queen Victoria's third and favourite son. In this first full biography, based on complete access to his papers, the author counterpoints the story of his remarkable public career with that of his private life.

'His career reads like a roll-call of Britain's imperial past ... '
THE SPECTATOR

ISBN 0 85683136 0 496pp b & w photos Index **£25 hb**